NATURE'S CYCLES

A FROG'S LIFE CYCLE

A.B. CLAMANT

NorwoodHouse Press

Cataloging-in-Publication Data

Names: Clamant, A.B., 1972-.
Title: A frog's life cycle / A.B. Clamant.
Description: Buffalo, NY : Norwood House Press, 2026. | Series: Nature's cycles | Includes glossary and index.
Identifiers: ISBN 9781978575585 (pbk.) | ISBN 9781978575592 (library bound) | ISBN 9781978575608 (ebook)
Subjects: LCSH: Frogs--Life cycles--Juvenile literature.
Classification: LCC QL668.E2 C536 2026 | DDC 597.8'9--dc23

Published in 2026 by
Norwood House Press
2544 Clinton Street
Buffalo, NY 14224

Designer: Rhea Magaro
Editor: Kim Thompson

Photo credits: Cover, p. 1 EVA SUKMA H/Shutterstock.com; p. 3 Harken Designs/Shutterstock.com; p. 5 Pixel Pulse Studio/Shutterstock.com; pp. 6, 21 Daniel Prudek/Shutterstock.com; p. 7 Krichevtseva/Shutterstock.com; p. 9 adamikarl/Shutterstock.com; p. 10 W. de Vries/Shutterstock.com; p. 15 Nick Greaves/Shutterstock.com; p. 17 Ken Griffiths/Shutterstock.com; p. 18 WildlifeWorld/Shutterstock.com; p. 19 Angelo Spillo/Shutterstock.com

Printed in the United States of America

CPSIA compliance information: Batch #CSNHP26: For further information contact Norwood House Press at 1-800-237-9932.

TABLE OF CONTENTS

Where Do Frogs Come From?

A frog uses legs to jump. A tadpole uses a tail to swim. The two things have nothing to do with each other, right? Wrong! They are both part of the amazing life **cycle** of frogs.

Floating Eggs

A frog begins life as an egg in the water. A female frog can lay thousands of eggs each spring. As she lays eggs, a male frog **fertilizes** them.

A mass of floating frog eggs is called frogspawn. The eggs look like black dots in clear jelly. The dots develop into **embryos**. They eat the jelly, which is full of **nutrients**.

Tadpole Time

After a few weeks, frog **larvae** hatch from the eggs. They are called tadpoles. For a few days, a tadpole stays still. It keeps eating its egg.

The tadpole grows a longer tail. It begins to swim around to find plants to eat. Its body is made for life in the water. It breathes through **gills**.

Big Changes

The tadpole begins a **metamorphosis** that will change it into a frog. It takes about 14 weeks.

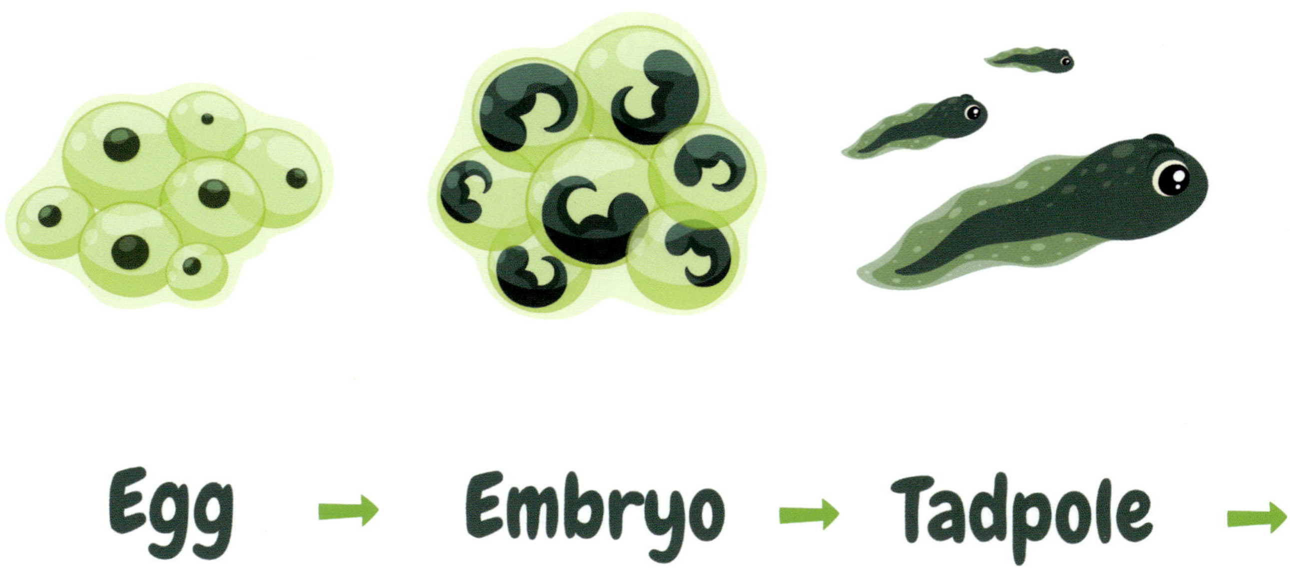

First, tiny back legs begin to grow. Then, front legs form. Skin grows over the gills. **Lungs** develop. The long tail shrinks.

In time, a tadpole’s tail and gills disappear. Now, it is a froglet. A froglet can come out of the water. It uses its legs to move on land. It uses its lungs to breathe.

Fully Froggy

A froglet gets bigger. It grows long, strong legs. It uses a long, sticky tongue to catch insects to eat. It is now an adult frog.

Frogs are **amphibians**. They live in water and on land. They are good jumpers, but they are also good swimmers. They never forget all the swimming practice they got as tadpoles!

Frogs live in shady places that are close to fresh water. They do not want their skin to dry out.

The Cycle Continues

Adult frogs are ready to **mate**. In the spring, females look for places to lay their eggs. The frog life cycle begins again.

Glossary

amphibians (am-FIB-ee-uhnz): cold-blooded animals that have backbones and that live part of their lives in water and part on land

cycle (SYE-kuhl): a series of events that repeat over and over in the same order

embryos (EM-bree-ohz): unborn babies

fertilizes (FUR-tuh-lize-is): provides the male parts that make a female's eggs able to grow into new life; joins male and female parts during mating

gills (gilz): organs near the mouth that fish and other animals use to breathe underwater

larvae (LAHR-vee): animals at an early stage of development when they look completely different from their parents

lungs (luhngz): baglike organs inside the chest that allow animals to breathe air

mate (mate): the pairing of a male and female to produce babies

metamorphosis (met-uh-MOR-fuh-sis): a series of major changes in form and appearance that some animals go through as they become adults; a transformation

nutrients (NOO-tree-uhntz): substances that living things need to grow and stay healthy, such as proteins, vitamins, and minerals

Thinking Questions

1. What is frogspawn?
2. What do tadpoles eat?
3. Describe the metamorphosis that changes a tadpole into a froglet.
4. What is an amphibian?
5. When do female frogs lay eggs?

Index

About the Author

A.B. Clamant is the author of several fact-filled books for kids. The daughter of two grade school teachers, she developed a love of children's books at an early age. When she's not writing, she is working on opening her own petting zoo, ABCs Animals. Her favorite foods are bread, fruit strips, and candy. A.B. Clamant lives in Springfield, Missouri, with her four cats: Monkey, Corky, Prissy, and Nelly.